ICE FISHING

BY SARA GREEN

BELLWETHER MEDIA • MINNEAPOLIS, MN

Jump into the cockpit and take flight with Pilot books. Your journey will take you on high-energy adventures as you learn about all that is wild, weird, fascinating, and fun!

This edition first published in 2014 by Bellwether Media, Inc.

No part of this publication may be reproduced in whole or in part without written permission of the publisher. For information regarding permission, write to Bellwether Media, Inc., Attention: Permissions Department, 5357 Penn Avenue South, Minneapolis, MN 55419.

Library of Congress Cataloging-in-Publication Data

Green, Sara, 1964-
 Ice Fishing / by Sara Green.
      pages cm – (Pilot: Outdoor Adventures)
 Includes bibliographical references and index.
 Summary: "Engaging images accompany information about ice fishing. The combination of high-interest subject matter and narrative text is intended for students in grades 3 through 7"– Provided by publisher.
 ISBN 978-1-62617-085-8 (hardcover : alk. paper)
 1. Ice fishing–Juvenile literature. I. Title.
 SH455.45.G74 2014
 799.12′2–dc23
                        2013035394

TABLE OF CONTENTS

ICE FISHING WITH FRIENDS

A cold winter wind blows across a frozen lake. Dozens of fish houses are set up on the ice. The chatter and laughter of ice anglers fill the air.

A group of friends trudge across the ice to one of the shelters. A small heater warms their fish house. Two chairs sit by a hole in the ice. One of the friends drops a baited fishing line into the hole and jigs it. Soon, she feels a tug. A fish took the bait! She pulls up a small bluegill and carefully unhooks it. It is very small, so she tosses it back into the lake.

Another friend returns from a second hole they drilled outside the fish house. She drops a yellow perch into a bucket. Soon, the bucket is filled with a variety of fish. Spending the day ice fishing with friends is so much fun!

Dedicated anglers look forward to the arrival of winter. It signals the start of ice fishing season! In this activity, anglers catch fish from frozen lakes through holes in the ice. They also fish in frozen ponds, rivers, and streams. Ice fishing is popular in many parts of the world. North American anglers ice fish in Canada and the northern United States. Europeans enjoy ice fishing in Finland, Norway, Russia, Ukraine and other northern countries.

People have been ice fishing for thousands of years. Early ice anglers caught fish to survive the long, cold winters. Today's anglers go ice fishing more for fun than necessity. Many enjoy being outside in nature, free from mosquitoes, flies, and other insects. Others want to spend time with friends and family in the shanty towns that spring up on the ice. Some ice anglers enjoy the challenge of catching the most or largest fish

ICE FISHING BASICS

Ice anglers catch the same fish as summer anglers. Panfish such as yellow perch and bluegills are favorites. Ice anglers also catch larger fish such as trout and walleye. Fish are less active in cold water. They will not swim far for food. Ice anglers must go to where the fish lurk. Fish stay in deep water in winter because it is warmer. Many seek shelter near submerged tree branches, rocks, or vegetation. Ice anglers use these clues to find the best fishing spots.

Ice anglers need just a few pieces of equipment to start fishing. They often use augers to make holes in the ice. Most anglers prefer power augers. They can cut through more than a foot (30 centimeters) of ice in less than a minute. Spuds test for ice thickness and chip ice from holes. A skimmer keeps the hole free

auger

Choosing the Best Spot

Panfish are often found in small, quiet lakes that have cattails, bulrushes, and other plants along the shoreline.

yellow perch

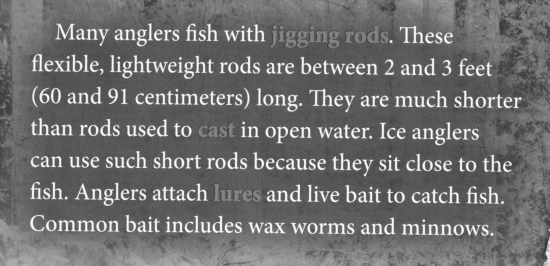

Many anglers fish with jigging rods. These flexible, lightweight rods are between 2 and 3 feet (60 and 91 centimeters) long. They are much shorter than rods used to cast in open water. Ice anglers can use such short rods because they sit close to the fish. Anglers attach lures and live bait to catch fish. Common bait includes wax worms and minnows.

lures

Many Tip-ups, Many Fish

Ice anglers who use jigging rods often set up a tip-up at a different hole. This allows them to try for more than one fish at a time.

tip-up

Another way to ice fish is to use tip-ups. In this method, a spool of fishing line is attached to a small pole. The angler baits the line and feeds it down the hole. A second pole lies across the hole to keep the first pole upright. A flag is attached to the top of the upright pole and tucked into the line. When a fish pulls on the line, the flag pops up. Now the angler knows a fish has taken the bait.

flasher

Ice anglers sometimes use special equipment to help them find fish beneath the ice. Underwater cameras allow anglers to see fish. A flasher tells anglers the depth of the water, the location of the lure, and if fish are swimming near it. If fish are absent at one depth, anglers move the fishing line to a different depth.

Some people prefer simpler methods and use only spears to ice fish. Spear fishing is the least common way to ice fish. This method is more traditional and takes more skill. Spear fishers must see the fish they want to catch. They cut large holes in the ice, usually with an ice saw or a chain saw. They fish from tents or small shelters called dark houses. These shelters block the light and help fishers see what is in the water.

Ice Fishing History

Early North Americans made spears from wood or animal bone. They chopped holes in the ice and used the spears to pierce fish that swam underneath them.

Ice anglers often sit inside small, moveable shelters called fish houses while they fish. They tow fish houses onto the thick ice to use throughout winter. In early spring, they bring them ashore before the ice melts. Fish houses protect anglers from the cold wind. Most have small heaters and chairs. Some of the largest fish houses have bathrooms, televisions, and beds!

Ice anglers can also use portable ice shelters. These tent-like shelters are easy to move, set up, and store. They are not as solid as fish houses, but they still block the wind. Anglers who like to fish on different lakes often use portable shelters.

Not all ice anglers use shelters. Many prefer to brave the cold weather. They head out with only a stool, fishing gear, and warm clothes. Then they enjoy the beauty of nature in silence.

SAFETY AND MANNERS ON THE ICE

Ice fishing is not a dangerous activity. However, ice anglers must follow some important safety guidelines. Before they step onto the ice, anglers must be sure the ice is thick enough to support their weight. The ice must be at least 4 inches (10 centimeters) thick for safe travel on foot. Ice must be 5 inches (13 centimeters) thick to support snowmobiles and all-terrain vehicles. It must be at least 12 inches (30 centimeters) thick to support the weight of cars or small trucks.

Ice anglers must always be aware of where ice is thick or thin. Clear or blue ice is often the safest. Gray, cloudy, or slushy ice may be weak and should be avoided.

Anglers should be prepared to help others in case of an accident. Everyone should bring ice rescue gear to help people who unexpectedly fall through the ice. This gear includes ice picks, life jackets, and extra blankets.

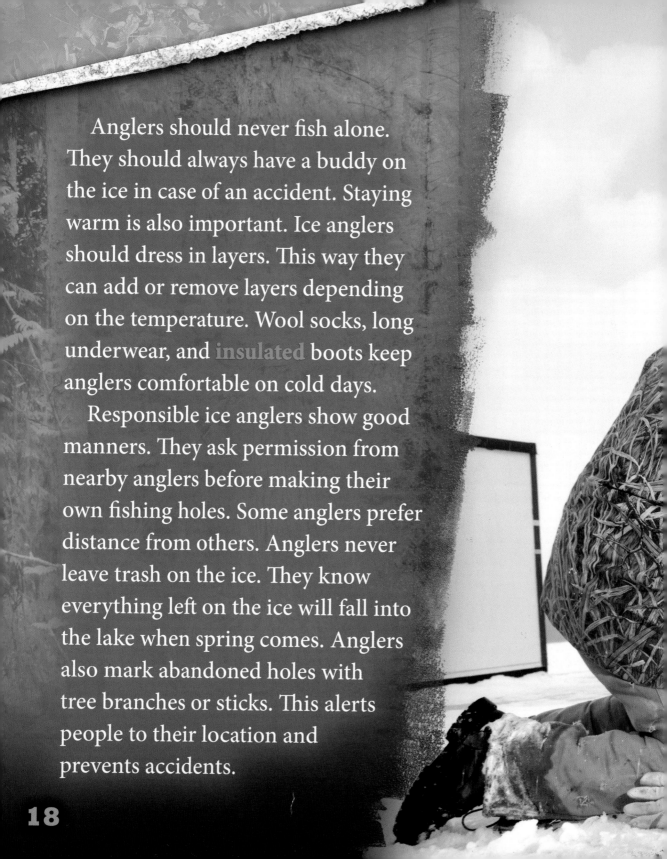

Anglers should never fish alone. They should always have a buddy on the ice in case of an accident. Staying warm is also important. Ice anglers should dress in layers. This way they can add or remove layers depending on the temperature. Wool socks, long underwear, and insulated boots keep anglers comfortable on cold days.

Responsible ice anglers show good manners. They ask permission from nearby anglers before making their own fishing holes. Some anglers prefer distance from others. Anglers never leave trash on the ice. They know everything left on the ice will fall into the lake when spring comes. Anglers also mark abandoned holes with tree branches or sticks. This alerts people to their location and prevents accidents.

Catch and Release

Ice anglers often release fish back into the water after they catch them. This helps keep the fish population stable and healthy.

ICE FISHING ADVENTURES IN MINNESOTA

Minnesota has more than 11,000 lakes. It is no surprise that ice fishing is one of the most popular winter activities! Around 150,000 fish houses are set up on Minnesota lakes every winter.

One of Minnesota's top ice fishing destinations is Lake of the Woods, a wilderness area that spans both Minnesota and Canada. Ice anglers travel from all over the world to fish for walleye in this scenic area.

Lake of the Woods

Minnesota

Gull Lake

N
W · E
S

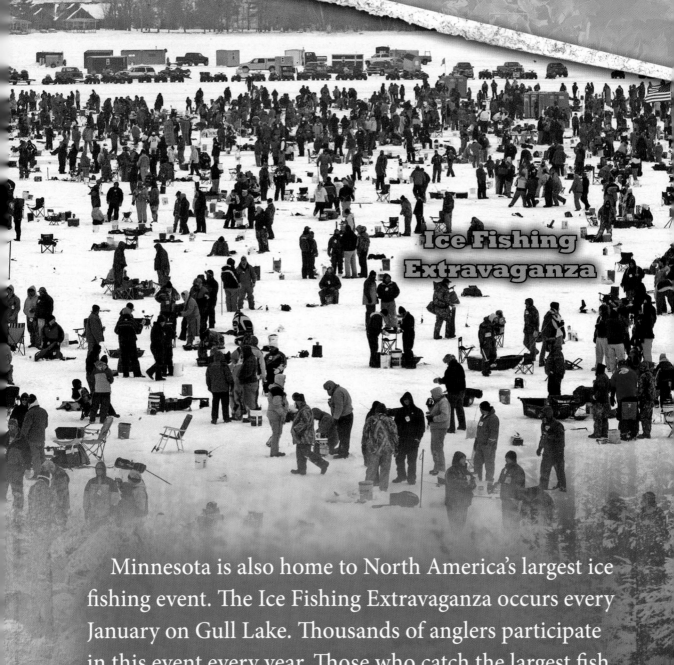

Ice Fishing Extravaganza

Minnesota is also home to North America's largest ice fishing event. The Ice Fishing Extravaganza occurs every January on Gull Lake. Thousands of anglers participate in this event every year. Those who catch the largest fish win money, cars, and other prizes. With so many lakes to choose from, ice anglers are sure to enjoy wintertime fishing in Minnesota!

GLOSSARY

anglers—people who fish

augers—tools shaped like corkscrews used for drilling holes in the ice

cast—to throw fishing line out into the water

fish houses—shelters used by ice anglers; fish houses are often made of wood or metal.

flasher—an electronic device used to measure depth and locate fish

insulated—covered with material that stops heat from escaping

jigging rods—short, lightweight fishing poles

jigs—jerks a fishing line up and down while fishing

lures—shiny, colorful pieces of fishing equipment that anglers use to attract fish

panfish—species of fish that are small enough to fit into a frying pan

portable—easily carried or moved

scenic—providing beautiful views of the natural surroundings

shanty towns—clusters of ice fishing shelters set up on a frozen lake

skimmer—a long-handled scoop with holes in it; a skimmer is used to clear ice from the hole.

snowmobiles—vehicles that are made to move quickly over snow

spuds—chisels used to chip ice and measure ice depth

traditional—relating to a custom, idea, or belief handed down from one generation to the next

wilderness—undeveloped land that is home to undisturbed plants and animals

TO LEARN MORE

At the Library

Green, Sara. *Freshwater Fishing*. Minneapolis, Minn.: Bellwether Media, Inc., 2013.

Omoth, Tyler. *Ice Fishing for Kids*. Mankato, Minn.: Capstone Press, 2013.

Schwartz, Tina P. *Ice Fishing*. New York, N.Y.: The Rosen Publishing Group, Inc., 2012.

On the Web

Learning more about ice fishing is as easy as 1, 2, 3.

1. Go to www.factsurfer.com.

2. Enter "ice fishing" into the search box.

3. Click the "Surf" button and you will see a list of related Web sites.

With factsurfer.com, finding more information is just a click away.

INDEX

The images in this book are reproduced through the courtesy of: Mitch Kezar/ Windigo Images, front cover; Johner Images/ Glow Images, pp. 4-5; James Smedley/ Alamy, pp. 6-7; Stephen McSweeny, p. 9 (left); photomim, p. 9 (right); Kalvis Kalsers, p. 10; Tom Thulen/ Windigo Images, p. 11; Craig Larcom/ Alamy, p. 12; Wayne R Bilenduke/ Getty Images, p. 13; Sophie Vigneault, p. 14; Brenda Carson, p. 15; LesPalenik, p. 16; Gero Breloer/ Newscom, p. 17; iofoto, pp. 18-19; Marlin Levison/ Newscom, pp. 20-21.